FOR YOUR HOME

DINING AREAS

FOR YOUR HOME

DINING AREAS

LISA SHOLNIK

FRIEDMAN/FAIRFAX
PUBLISHERS

Dedication

For Caroline, Alexander, Anastasia, and Theodora, whose legacy lies in the dining room.
May you all host the family repasts one day.

Acknowledgments

Thank you to the staff at Michael Friedman Publishing Group, particularly my talented editor,
Hallie Einhorn, whose input and initiative contributed greatly to this book. I wish to also
express special thanks to Margaret Visser, the author of "Much Depends on Dinner," "The Rituals
of Dinner," and "The Way We Are," whom I have interviewed on many occasions for
stories and called upon once again in writing this book.

A FRIEDMAN/FAIRFAX BOOK

© 1996 by Michael Friedman Publishing Group, Inc.

Library of Congress Cataloging-in-Publication Data

Skolnik, Lisa.
Dining areas / Lisa Skolnik.
p. cm. – (For your home)
Includes index.
ISBN 1-56799-282-X (pbk.)
1. Dining rooms–Design and construction. 2. Interior decoration.
I. Title. II. Series.
TX855.S57 1995
643'.4–dc20   95-48066
                                    CIP

Editor: Hallie Einhorn
Art Director: Lynne Yeamans
Designer: Jan Melchior
Photography Editor: Wendy Missan
Production Director: Karen Matsu Greenberg

Color separations by Fine Arts Repro House Co., Ltd.
Printed in China by Leefung-Asco Printers Ltd.

For bulk purchases and special sales, please contact:
Friedman/Fairfax Publishers
Attention: Sales Department
15 West 26th Street
New York, New York 10010
212/685-6610 FAX 212/685-1307

Table of Contents

INTRODUCTION

The ritual of eating together has to be one of the most common—yet complex—activities mankind has yet devised. It gives us the opportunity to spend time with our families, rest from work, and socialize with friends. In fact, many of the events in our lives revolve around food, from prosaic family meals to milestones marked by celebratory repasts to savory holiday feasts. These are instances that we will always remember.

Given the monumental importance that eating has in our lives, it is not surprising that all sorts of areas have evolved in our homes to accommodate this activity. The sites at which we dine are many and varied, and some residences have more than one area designated for this purpose. There are formal dining rooms, eat-in kitchens, quaint breakfast nooks, and dining areas carved out of libraries; the great room, a relatively new innovation that is supplanting the formal living room, often incorporates an eating area; and many of us have also found spaces on our terraces and patios for dining.

But given the history of dining, it is clear that society as a whole has made the most of the experience only in contemporary times. Although dining was an extraordinary affair for the upper classes during previous centuries, it was a far more humble experience for the masses. Upper-class males reclined on couches while dining in ancient Assyria, Samaria, Phoenicia, Greece, and Rome; this practice limited fine dining to groups that were small and exclusive, since not many couches could fit in a room. And at the beginning of the European Middle Ages, an aristocratic household would typically have a spacious central hall where servants would eat while watched by their lord. The master would eventually withdraw to dine in private with his companions, and the practice of eating in chambers away from the lower orders evolved.

Rooms designed for the sole purpose of dining were not built into middle-class homes until the seventeenth century. When this type of space evolved, furnishings specific to the room quickly followed suit. For the first time,

Opposite: WITH LUSH FLORAL SLIPCOVERS OVER HALF OF ITS CHAIRS, THIS COLONIAL DINING ROOM SPORTS A SUMMERY LOOK THROUGHOUT THE SEASONS. AN AIRY CHANDELIER, A BOUNTIFUL FLORAL CENTERPIECE, AND BLUE-AND-WHITE CHECKERED DRAPES COMPLETE THE PRETTY PICTURE AND MAKE DINING HERE SEEM LIKE A FORMAL INDOOR PICNIC.

distinctive tables that were stationary, and meant only for eating, were built. Prior to that, trestles and boards were constantly being set up and dismantled in whatever space could accommodate them. These temporary arrangements were adorned, however, with splendid cloths—a procedure, in fact, that originated the practice of dressing the table.

Along with the dining room came many other innovations, such as place settings, silver, glassware and linens as we know them today, elegant dining chairs, sideboards, buffets, breakfronts, and cupboards. The concept that functional objects could also be decorative, even fanciful, began to take hold, and soon whole industries revolving around the accoutrements of dining sprang up. By the mid-nineteenth century, the dining room was laden with layers of elaborate gear. There were pieces of cutlery for every kind of food, as well as plates, serving pieces, and glasses in every size for every imaginable course. As specialized forms evolved for cheese, fruit, fish, shellfish, meat, salad, and soup, a place setting of silver or china could include a dozen different pieces. Cabinetry to store these pieces proliferated and even became a necessity for a well-appointed room.

It is important to remember, though, that all these accessories were designed to grace the dining table, which was—

Above: DESPITE THE FACT THAT THIS ADOBE ROOM HAS RUSTIC BEAMED CEILINGS AND A TERRA-COTTA TILE FLOOR, IT IS FURNISHED WITH QUEEN ANNE CHAIRS, A SIMPLE PROVINCIAL TRESTLE TABLE, AN EMPIRE LOVE SEAT, AND BAROQUE WROUGHT-IRON FIXTURES EMBELLISHED WITH FLAMBOYANT CRYSTAL BALLS—ALL OF WHICH PROVIDE A WELCOME SURPRISE. THE ROOM HAS AN AGELESS QUALITY, SEEMING CONTEMPORARY AND ARCHAIC AT THE SAME TIME DUE TO THE ALMOST MAGICAL BLEND OF ELEMENTS.

and still is—the focal point of a dining area. Since everything revolves around this one crucial piece of furniture, it has traditionally been a substantial—and special—piece.

The first stationary dining tables, crafted in heavy dark woods polished to perfection, reflected the style of their day. They were usually rectangular, both to accommodate strict hierarchical seating distinctions and to suit the oblong shapes of the rooms in those days. The furnishings that surrounded the dining table matched in terms of style and scale, for the dining room was a very formal space. In fact, it retained its starched demeanor until quite recently, when the nature of formal dining spaces changed and contemporary design popularized the concept of "the big blend."

Today, dining tables continue to take center stage, but they no longer adhere to one specific shape or style. Moreover, they are not always placed in formal spaces. Personal preference is far more important than social convention; thus, there are no rules to dictate the style and dimensions of our tables. If anything, taste and common sense help determine the type of table chosen. Rectangular tables work better for large groups, while those that are round are far more democratic. Plus tables that expand and contract, such as those with leaves or clever foldout surfaces, provide far more versatility than tables that are truly stationary.

And just as personal preference leads us to pick certain tables, it leads us to array our dining areas as we please. Many factors influence this process, starting with the size of the space, how it has to function, and an individual's taste and sense of decorum. Some dining areas are still formal, while others are casual, relaxed, and even full of surprise. It is possible to recreate a perfect period room, be it a stately Federal or Empire interior or a sleek Art Deco or Modernist milieu, or produce a fantastic space that incorporates all sorts of decorative elements in an eclectic blend. Somewhere in between fall rooms that reflect regional or ethnic styling.

Ultimately, a dining area must be an inviting space designed for sharing, since eating is an activity that often takes place in the company of others. Dining is an entertaining and fulfilling social experience, and the setting for such an endeavor should be comfortable, engaging, and ideally, stimulate the appetite and conversation. Given such a space, who wouldn't want to linger around a table for hours at a time?

Formal Dining

In 1879, an anonymous aristocrat wrote in an English manners book that "dinner parties rank first among all entertainments." Considering the marvelous times to be had—both intellectually and gastronomically—around a table, this observation is astute. Moreover, it reminds us that a dinner party demands a stage of its own on which it can unfold.

The notion of a singular room devoted entirely to dining became most firmly established as a standard in the European household during the second half of the nineteenth century, at just about the same time that this blue blood was advocating the merits of the dinner party. It was a fortuitous development, for what better way is there to enjoy the diversion of dining than in an alluring room outfitted for the occasion?

A grand table is like a mannequin that can be dressed many ways. Thanks to its proportions, it already anchors the room, but it receives its character from the furnishings and accessories around it. Pristine linens bring it starched propriety, while vibrant fabrics make it festive. Chairs add attitude, whether it is the refinement offered by traditional Chippendales or the "edge" induced by avant-garde designs. Other furnishings, such as breakfronts and sideboards, remind us of the utilitarian aspects of dining and its many necessary accessories.

Enjoying a dinner party in a formal dining room is only half the fun. Indeed, picking and choosing all the accoutrements for the space can be just as mesmerizing.

Opposite: STARK SIMPLICITY MAKES THIS ROOM STUNNING, ALLOWING ITS CAREFULLY PRESERVED ARCHITECTURAL ELEMENTS TO TAKE CENTER STAGE. THE WAINSCOTING, CORNICES, AND WINDOW CASEMENTS LITERALLY JUMP OFF THE WALLS IN PURE WHITE, WHILE THE FLAT PARTS OF THE SURFACE ARE GIVEN DEPTH WITH A COAT OF DEEP GRAY PAINT. FURNISHING THIS SPECTACULAR SPACE WITH JUST A TABLE AND CHAIRS SHOWS REMARKABLE RESTRAINT, BUT PAYS OFF WITH THE DRAMATIC IMPACT EVOKED BY SUCH MINIMALISM. **Above:** A FORMAL SEVENTEENTH-CENTURY DINING ROOM IN THE ENGLISH COUNTRYSIDE WOULD HAVE LOOKED VERY MUCH LIKE THIS, RIGHT DOWN TO THE LOW CEILINGS, BANISTER-BACK CHAIRS, ORIENTAL CARPET, AND ELABORATE CANDELABRA. THANKS TO THE FIREPLACE, THE SPACE FEELS IMPOSING AND INTIMATE AT THE SAME TIME—A RARE BALANCE IN ANY SETTING.

Opposite: THIS AIRY DINING ROOM TAKES MUCH FROM CLASSIC REGENCY STYLING, STARTING WITH THE DINING TABLE AND CHAIRS. SINCE ALL PIECES FROM THIS PERIOD HAVE MUCH IN COMMON, MIXING TWO TYPES OF CHAIRS LOOKS QUITE ELEGANT INSTEAD OF DISCORDANT, AND EVEN GIVES THE SETTING A DISCREET TOUCH OF EXCITEMENT. THE WALLS BORROW THE MOST FROM THE PERIOD, WHEN LARGE PLAIN SURFACES WERE FREQUENTLY PAINTED A SINGLE COLOR AND COVERED WITH SUBTLE STENCILED PATTERNS. HOWEVER, THE USE OF A COORDINATING BORDER EMBLAZONED WITH EPIGRAMS TRANSPORTS THE ROOM INTO TODAY'S TIMES.

Above: EVEN THOUGH IT IS TUCKED AWAY IN A CORNER, A SURREALISTIC GRANDFATHER CLOCK STANDS WATCH IN THIS ROOM AND GIVES IT ATTITUDE. WHILE OTHER ELEMENTS APPEAR AT FIRST GLANCE TO BE MINIMAL, THE SPACE ACTUALLY EMPLOYS SPECIAL PIECES TO MAXIMUM EFFECT. DESPITE SEEMINGLY STRAIGHTFORWARD LINES, THE DINING SET RELATES TO THE CLOCK WITH ITS SUBTLY ECCENTRIC CHAIRS. AND A WHITE VASE THAT ECHOES THE CHAIRS' FAN-SHAPED BACKS SERVES AS A COUNTERPOINT TO THE ALL-BLACK TABLE SURFACE. FINALLY, A CONTEMPORARY PAINTING THAT COMBINES THE HUES OF THE ROOM PULLS THE VARIOUS COMPONENTS TOGETHER.

Above: A WOOD DINING SET WITH STRONG, CHUNKY LINES LOOKS HIGHLY REFINED AS A "BLOND." ALTHOUGH IT TAKES ITS CUES FROM THE SENSIBLE AND SERIOUS MISSION MOVEMENT, A WARDROBE OF RUFFLED SKIRTS IMBUES IT WITH A TOUCH OF WIT AND SOFTENS ITS SOBER PROFILE. THE SET PROVIDES AN INTERESTING CONTRAST TO THE DARK WOOD FLOOR AND TROLLEY. **Right:** BOLD GEOMETRIC SHAPES PUNCTUATE THIS ROOM, GIVING IT A COMMANDING AIR. BUT BILLOWING DRAPES, UPHOLSTERED CHAIRS, AND FRESH FLOWERS TONE DOWN THE SHARP ANGLES THAT DOMINATE THE SPACE, MAKING IT SEEM A LITTLE MORE DELICATE.

Opposite: IN THIS SURREAL DIN-
ING ROOM, CARICATURES OF TRADITION
MINGLE WITH THE REAL THING, PRODUC-
ING A REMARKABLY SOPHISTICATED AND
COHESIVE EFFECT. THE TENETS OF
QUEEN ANNE STYLING ARE STRETCHED
IN THE EXAGGERATED LINES OF THE
BLOND WOOD PIECES, WHICH CLEARLY
DO NOT TAKE THEMSELVES TOO SERI-
OUSLY: TALL POTTERY POKES OUT OVER
THE TOP OF THE CABINET, THE CHAIR
LOOKS LOPSIDED, AND THE FRAME LACKS
A PICTURE. BUT WHEN PAIRED WITH AU-
THENTIC ANTIQUE ELEMENTS—NAMELY A
VICTORIAN SPIRAL-LEG TABLE BASE, EMPIRE
CHAIRS, AND A PRIMITIVE BENCH—THESE
PIECES MAKE THE ROOM ENGAGING.

Right: A BREATHTAKING ALCOVE
OUTFITTED IN ICY WHITE MAKES A SPEC-
TACULAR SPOT FOR DINING, ESPECIALLY
WHEN BLESSED WITH THE STUNNING
BACKDROP OF A LAKE. IN THIS CASE,
THOUGH, THE VISTA WAS ACTUALLY A
MIXED BLESSING SINCE IT RENDERED THE
SPACE SOMEWHAT COLD AND PRISTINE.
EASY CHAIRS PLACED AROUND THE TABLE
MAKE THE NOOK MORE COZY, WHILE
PALE GREEN PAINT PROVIDES AN
ADDITIONAL SOFTENING EFFECT.

Left, top: This tiny dining alcove sports many elements of Baroque styling. The massive form of the armoire, with its swelling curves and lacquered veneer, dominates the room, which is accentuated by rod-hung curtains (an innovation of the period). To offset the room's small size and give it the illusion of spaciousness, the far wall is paneled with mirrors while the other walls, along with the ceiling, are painted an airy shade of yellow (also popular during the Baroque period). But a clever mix of other period pieces, accented by Indonesian textiles, brings this room into the era of jet travel.

Left, bottom: This Tex-Mex milieu owes much to other influences. The chairs are pure Adirondack, the harvest table is right out of the Midwest, and the lamp is Arts and Crafts. But the Native American textile and pottery, coupled with an antique Mexican serape and a beamed ceiling, cement the ambience of the room as Southwestern.

Opposite: It is hard to imagine a wonderful room totally washed in orange, but this dining area manages to be earthy, warm, witty, and undeniably that hue all at the same time. Part of the success of the milieu is owed to the mellow tone-on-tone approach employed in the palette, which ranges from a sunny tangerine to a rich terra-cotta. But other sly devices, such as comic slipcovers that make the chairs look like court jesters and a flashy fixture with faux-skin shades, clue us in on this room's real aim, which is to entertain.

Above: HERE, REGAL SPANISH COLONIAL FURNISHINGS ARE ENHANCED BY STARK WHITE ADOBE WALLS, WHICH SHOW OFF THE INKY MAHOGANY PIECES TO PERFECTION. A VIVID TRADITIONAL NATIVE AMERICAN RUG ADDS COLOR TO THE SETTING, WHILE THE CEILING, WITH ITS DARK WOOD BEAMS AND STENCILED GEOMETRIC MOTIF, FUSES THE CULTURAL ASPECTS OF THE SPACE. HOWEVER, THE ROOM IS NOT WITHOUT ITS IDIOSYNCRASIES: NEOCLASSICAL DORIC COLUMNS FLANKING THE DOOR ARE TOTALLY OUT OF PLACE BUT WORK, THANKS TO THEIR MOTTLED TONES AND THE CARVED MAHOGANY CORNICE THEY SUPPORT. **Opposite:** HERE, ELEGANT UPHOLSTERED DINING CHAIRS WITH BOX-PLEATED SKIRTS BRING SOBRIETY TO AN AUDACIOUS ALUMINUM TABLE, JUST AS WHITE GLOVES WOULD TONE DOWN A SHOWY PAIR OF PATENT LEATHER SHOES. OTHER SPLASHY ELEMENTS—NAMELY THE CHAMPAGNE STAND AND THE BRIGHT SHADE OF RED SANDWICHED BETWEEN THE WAINSCOTING AND MOLDING—DO NOT APPEAR OVERWHELMING THANKS TO CAREFUL EDITING AND BALANCE.

Opposite: EXCESS REIGNS SUPREME IN THIS ROOM, WHICH IS STARTLING ON ACCOUNT OF ITS BOLD USE OF COLOR, PATTERN, AND PROPORTION. MASSIVE CHINOISERIE PIECES, SUCH AS THE BREAKFRONT AND DINING SET, ARE SURROUNDED BY A COCOON OF COLORS AND PATTERNS THAT PLAY OFF THE RED AND GOLD TONES IN THESE FURNISHINGS. THE WALL TREATMENT, WHICH CONSISTS OF A PATCHWORK APPROACH THAT FUSES SQUARES OF DIFFERENT-PATTERNED PAPERS ALL ON THE SAME SURFACE, IS A MOST NOVEL DEVICE THAT CAN BE DUPLICATED IN OTHER SETTINGS.

Right: COMBINING A QUILTED TABLE SKIRT, TEXTURED SLIPCOVERS, AND FLOCKED CANVAS DRAPES WAS A DARING MOVE THAT PAID OFF. EACH OF THE TEXTILES IS RICH IN ITS OWN RIGHT, BUT TOGETHER THEY BECOME DOWNRIGHT OPULENT AS THEY PLAY OFF ONE ANOTHER. THIS SAME LOOK CAN BE DUPLICATED WITH SIMILAR FABRICS THAT ARE FAR MORE HUMBLE, SUCH AS A MOVER'S QUILT OR A PRINTED CHINTZ.

Left, bottom: IN THIS FAN-TASTICAL NEO-GOTHIC SETTING, THE BUILT-IN WALNUT CABINET, WHICH WAS DESIGNED TO RESEMBLE THE EXTERIOR OF A GOTHIC BUILDING, IS ACTUALLY A STRUCTURAL DEVICE THAT HIDES THE ROOM'S ONLY WINDOW, WHICH OVERLOOKS AN UNAPPEAL-ING FIRE ESCAPE. NATURAL LIGHT, HOWEVER, IS PERMITTED TO SHINE IN FROM THE GLASS EXPANSE AT THE TOP OF THE UNIT, AND A TROMPE L'OEIL SKY COVERS THE CEILING, THEREBY OPENING UP THE SPACE AND MASKING THE FACT THAT THE CEILING IS ACTUALLY QUITE LOW. SINCE THIS BUSY BACKDROP CALLS FOR VERY LITTLE FURNITURE, ONLY THE BARE NECESSITIES HAVE BEEN INCORPORATED. A GOTHIC-STYLE TABLE, WHICH USED TO BE THE PROP OF AN OPERA COMPANY, WAS DIS-TRESSED TO LOOK LIKE THE REAL THING, WHILE TAPESTRY FROM A FABRIC STORE WAS MADE INTO A REGAL TABLECLOTH. TURN-OF-THE-CENTURY FRENCH METAL GARDEN CHAIRS MAKE A PERFECT COUNTER-POINT TO THE MASSIVE PIECE.

Above: EMPIRE ROOMS WERE DRENCHED IN GILT AND LUXURIOUSLY SWATHED WITH GLEAMING SILK AND TAFFETA TO EMULATE MAGNIFICENT MILITARY TENTS. THIS DINING ROOM, WITH ITS DRAPED WALLS, LAVISH GOLD PASSEMENTERIE, HUGE GILT-FRAMED MIRROR, AND RUG EMBLAZONED WITH MEDALLIONS, RECREATES THE PERIOD SO STUNNINGLY THAT THE SIMPLICITY OF THE DINING SET GOES UNNOTICED. THOUGH CLEARLY NOT EMPIRE, THE TABLE AND CHAIRS FIT RIGHT IN AND ARE MADE FAR MORE GRAND BY THEIR OPULENT SURROUNDINGS.

Above: NOTHING CONVEYS THE ESSENCE OF STYLE BETTER THAN A SKILLFUL BLEND. HERE, AN ODD COUPLING BECOMES A STELLAR MATCH, AS A SPACE FITTED WITH SLEEK CONTEMPORARY BUILT-IN CABINETRY HOUSES A MASSIVE VICTORIAN DINING TABLE. THE SUBTLETY OF THE ROOM, WITH ITS UNDERSTATED BUT QUIETLY ELEGANT VENEERS, IS NOT ONLY BALANCED BY THE FLASHY TABLE—IT THRIVES ON THE FLAMBOYANCE. SPARTAN WOVEN RATTAN CHAIRS AROUND THE TABLE PROVIDE JUST THE RIGHT COUNTERPOINT, BRINGING THE STRIKING PIECE UP-TO-DATE.

Left: A BUILT-IN MISSION-STYLE SIDEBOARD DID NOT INHIBIT THE DESIGNER OF THIS ROOM, WHO CONTRASTED ETHEREAL TROMPE L'OEIL MURALS OF THE ITALIAN COUNTRYSIDE AND A ROMANTIC AUBUSSON RUG WITH CONTEMPORARY ITALIAN AVANT-GARDE FURNISHINGS. THE GLASS TABLE AND ITS ACCOMPANYING CHAIRS ARE SO SPARE AND MINIMAL THAT THEY ALLOW THE BEAUTY OF THE RUG TO SHINE THROUGH. ALTHOUGH THE COMPONENTS OF THIS ROOM ARE DISPARATE, THEY HAVE BEEN HARMONIOUSLY WOVEN TOGETHER.

Above: A ROOM CAN SAY "COUNTRY" BUT STILL SPEAK THE SAME LANGUAGE AS ITS PEERS IN SLICKER SETTINGS.

HERE, THE ARCHITECTURAL ELEMENTS OF A NEW ENGLAND DINING ROOM GIVE OFF A GENERAL SENSE OF COUNTRY STYLING.

BUT OUTFITTING THE SPACE WITH TRAPPINGS FROM THE GEORGIAN PERIOD—NAMELY A SPLENDID BURNISHED DINING SET IN THE

CHIPPENDALE FASHION, A GRACEFUL CHANDELIER, AND AN ORIENTAL CARPET—DRESSES UP THE FOLKSY BRICK-LINED HEARTH.

THESE FURNISHINGS WOULD BE DIGNIFIED IN ANY SPACE; HERE, THEY MAKE THE DINING ROOM DECOROUS.

INFORMAL DINING

While some find eating to be one of life's greatest pleasures, there is a compulsory side to this activity: we either do it or die. So eat we do, day in and day out, in a multitude of informal settings. Some people steal meals in a kitchen alcove, while others sit down with the whole household in spacious rooms. The challenge is not necessarily finding a spot for routine meals; it is making an eating environment inviting and comfortable enough for daily use.

There are many ways to make an informal dining area much more than merely routine. A good place to start is with a spectacular table, which does not have to be costly, ceremonious, or even conventional. The humble harvest table thrives just as well in an informal setting as

do its showier brethren, and there is even room for dining surfaces that are atypical or eccentric. What matters is how the table works in its environment. Can it accommodate all the members of a family; does it suit the space; and is it going to be easy to maintain?

Other basics to bring to an informal dining area include comfortable chairs, a manageable circulation pattern, plenty of storage, and good lighting. But it is the extras that make the space great. An imaginative paint job goes a long way in making the room engaging, as do novel fabric treatments, such as slipcovers or a table skirt. Sometimes that one special touch makes the otherwise mundane space we eat in every day remarkable.

Opposite: Representing simpler times, a beautifully weathered harvest table can imbue a room with the innocence of a past era. Here, a quaint fringed cloth deftly covers only part of such a table, allowing the natural beauty of the wood to be enjoyed. Brightly painted chairs, manifesting a slightly weathered look that blends in readily with the rustic table, add a splash of festivity to the setting. A subdued floral carpet and subtly stenciled walls further enhance the modest table without overshadowing it.

Above: A beautiful Native American rug and intricate moldings give this space a serious demeanor, but white wicker chairs and tablecloths resembling picnic blankets help the room to "lighten up." These playful elements liberate the room from the constraints of adhering to a specific style, thereby lending the area a carefree spirit.

Above: EIGHTEENTH-CENTURY COUNTRY STYLING HAS BEEN EVOKED WITH STUNNING RESULTS IN THIS INVITING MILIEU, WHERE AN ABUNDANCE OF WINDOWS GIVES THE SPACE A REFRESHING FEELING. THE FURNISHINGS, ALL OF WHICH ARE NEW EXCEPT FOR THE PLANK DINING TABLE, HAVE BEEN CHOSEN WITH EXTREME ACUMEN TO CREATE AN OVERALL PERIOD LOOK. TWO-TONE WINDSOR CHAIRS, COMPLETE WITH CONTEMPORARY FLOURISHES ON THE ARMS, AND A CHANDELIER WITH SOFTENING SHADES ADD THE SAME KIND OF ELEGANCE TO THE ROOM THAT ORIGINALS WOULD. **Opposite:** THANKS TO A MINIMAL USE OF FURNISHINGS AND COLOR, THE ARCHITECTURAL SPLENDOR OF THIS SPACE GRABS CENTER STAGE. THE FEW PIECES THAT ARE EMPLOYED MAKE KEY CONTRIBUTIONS TO THE SETTING: UNUSUAL WHITE CHAIRS WITH CASTORS, WHICH ADD TO THE CASUAL TONE OF THE ROOM, BLEND IN WITH THE BRIGHT WHITENESS OF THE SPACE'S STRUCTURAL ELEMENTS, WHILE THE CHAIRS' CURVED BACKS PROVIDE CONTRAST TO THE CRISP ARCHITECTURE. MEANWHILE, THE PALE WOOD TABLE BLENDS SEAMLESSLY INTO THE FLOOR AND BEARS A DARK BORDER THAT MIRRORS THE ONE BELOW.

Above, left: THIS SUNNY DINING AREA DEFINES CASUAL ELEGANCE IN EVERY WAY. A WOODEN FARM TABLE PAIRED WITH LINEN-SLIPCOVERED CHAIRS AND DRESSED WITH FINE TABLE LINENS, ORNATE FLATWARE, AND SILVER CANDLESTICKS IS AT ONCE RELAXED YET READY FOR COMPANY. LIKEWISE, THE ORIENTAL RUG ADDS A MORE FORMAL TOUCH THAT IS BALANCED BY THE SIMPLICIITY OF THE RUSTIC CHANDELIER, CURTAIN TREATMENT, AND WOODEN CHEST OF DRAWERS.

Above, right: A FEW SIMPLE BUT UNUSUAL FABRIC TREATMENTS ENHANCE THIS DINING AREA. BOX PLEATS ADD A TOUCH OF WHIMSY TO THE STRAIGHTFORWARD SLIPCOVERS, AND A DIAPHANOUS DRAPE BRINGS ADDITIONAL SOFTNESS TO THE DECOR. A RICE-PAPER FIXTURE CASTING A BURNISHED GLOW ECHOES THE SHAPE OF THE TABLE BELOW AS WELL AS THE HUE OF THE GOSSAMER WINDOW COVERING. COMBINED, THESE ELEMENTS CREATE AN INTIMATE AND NURTURING ENVIRONMENT.

Left: A SUBTLE MOTIF CAN
DEMONSTRATE TREMENDOUS DECO-
RATIVE POWER. HERE, A SIMPLE
CARVED STAR-IN-A-CIRCLE DESIGN
APPEARS ON THE BACKBOARD OF
EACH CHAIR, AS WELL AS ON
DECORATIVE BRACKETS EMBELLISHING
THE CORNERS OF THE ROOM.
CREATING AN OVERALL TEX-MEX
APPEAL, THE MOTIF SETS THE TONE
FOR THE REST OF THE FURNISHINGS.
SUDDENLY ELEMENTS THAT COULD
REFLECT SEVERAL DIFFERENT STYLES—
SUCH AS A COLLECTION OF POTTERY,
A TILED HARVEST TABLE, AND A
WEATHERED CUPBOARD—SEEM
DECIDEDLY SOUTHWESTERN.

Opposite: IN THIS COZY DINING ROOM, THE TABLE WAS THE INSPIRATION FOR THE SURROUNDING DECOR, WHICH BOASTS A SUPERB FAUX PAINT JOB THAT EMULATES THE TABLE'S BEAUTIFULLY VARIEGATED MARBLE SURFACE. SIMPLE WOOD CHAIRS AND A SISAL RUG TONE DOWN THE OPULENCE AND FORMALITY SUGGESTED BY MARBLE, WHILE A BOLD SAUCERLIKE FIXTURE AND FRENCH DOORS BOASTING A DYNAMIC SHADE OF TURQUOISE ADD A SENSE OF ADVENTURE.

Left: THERE IS A DEFINITE ART TO MINING THE ORDINARY NOOKS AND CRANNIES OF A HOME. HERE, A BAY WINDOW BECOMES THE PERFECT SITE FOR A DINING SPOT. THE ASTUTE USE OF A BANQUETTE MAXIMIZES SEATING POTENTIAL, WHICH IS ENHANCED STILL FURTHER BY A CLEVERLY DESIGNED DROP-LEAF TABLE THAT CAN BE OPENED UP TO COMFORTABLY ACCOMMODATE SEVERAL MORE DINERS. CUSHIONS DECKED OUT IN PRIMARY COLORS PROVIDE BRIGHT ACCENTS FOR THE ALL-WHITE SURROUNDINGS, MAKING THIS A CHEERY SPACE IN WHICH TO DINE. **Above:** TURNING TO NOVEL SOURCES FOR DINING ROOM COMPONENTS IS ONE WAY TO COME UP WITH INTRIGUING FURNISHINGS. HERE, THE TOP OF AN OLD POOL TABLE, STRIPPED TO ITS VERY BONES, BECOMES AN EVERYDAY DINING TABLE WITH A FAR-FROM-EVERYDAY LOOK. STAINLESS STEEL CHAIRS HEIGHTEN THE TABLE'S HIGH-TECH AURA, BUT A WOOD FLOOR, SCONCES WRAPPED IN STRAW "HULA SKIRTS," AND A COLORFUL BENCH TOPPED WITH A SERAPE ADD WARMTH AND TEXTURE TO THE ROOM. AN ABSTRACT TRIANGULAR CENTERPIECE BEARS RESEMBLANCE TO A RACK OF POOL BALLS.

Opposite: An informal dining room can host a formal gathering when dressed with the right accessories. Here, a casual space boasting wrought-iron chairs and a basic yet quaint blue-and-white color scheme gets dressed up with the help of a champagne bucket, festive china, and gold-rimmed glasses that add just the right amount of polish and flair for an evening of entertaining.

Right, top: Casual dining areas can also be gussied up with the help of textiles, which are highly flexible and available in myriad patterns, styles, and colors. Here, a plain underskirt masks massive wooden legs, while a lacy tablecloth and a profuse centerpiece of dried flowers spruce up the simple setting. Even the sturdy painted wooden chairs seem more ornate next to the dressed-up table.

Right, bottom: This snug dining area, carved out of an enclosed porch, thinks big but is actually relatively small. Thanks to a couchlike banquette, several diners can sit along the far side of the table and enjoy the same kind of comfort as their companions relaxing in oversize, cushioned wicker chairs. The banquette allows the dining area to appropriate less floor space yet still look roomy.

KINGAN'S
"LA PERLA"

DELIZIOSISSIMO · DI FAMA MONDIALE

Opposite: SLAT-STYLE PINE PANELS SEEM SO FAMILIAR AND ALL-AMERICAN THAT THEY ALMOST LULL ONE INTO OVERLOOKING THE ECCENTRICITIES OF THIS ENTICING DINING AREA: THE GILDED CHANDELIER IS COUPLED WITH GOTHICLIKE LANTERNS; AN UNUSUALLY LARGE MOLDING TOPS THE WALLS AND BORDERS THE CEILING; AND MISMATCHED CHAIRS SURROUND THE TABLE. A COLLECTION OF FIESTAWARE, AN OLD ADVERTISEMENT, AND A CLOCK FACE RIMMED IN BLUE NEON COMBINE TO CREATE AN INTERESTING ARRAY OF COLORS IN THIS IDIOSYNCRATIC SPACE, WHICH HAS AN ENDEARING SENSE OF CHARM. **Right:** INSTEAD OF GOING FOR CONTRAST IN THIS PANELED DINING ROOM, THE DESIGNER USED A PANOPLY OF COORDINATING WOODS TO MAKE A DRAMATIC IMPACT. THE LOGS OF THE ADIRONDACK-STYLE CHAIRS AND DINING TABLE HARMONIZE READILY WITH THE SUPPORT BEAMS OF THE HOUSE, WHILE AT THE SAME TIME PROVIDE AN INTERESTING FOIL FOR THE POLISHED PANELING. MOREOVER, THEY MIRROR THE SURROUNDING FOREST, WHICH BECOMES PART OF THE DINING EXPERIENCE THANKS TO WINDOWS LEFT ALLURINGLY BARE. A CUT STEEL FIXTURE HANGING OVERHEAD APPROPRIATELY EVOKES A FOREST SCENE AND SERVES AS A FASCINATING CONVERSATION PIECE.

Opposite: Despite a Southwestern demeanor, this room is rooted in Mission styling. The chairs, lighting fixture, and pilaster are perfect examples of this form and are highlighted by touches of country styling. Nonetheless, the Adirondack dining table, a trading blanket, and a cowhide rug shine through to steal the show.

Below: An imaginative paint job, part sophisticated and part just plain kitsch, gives the Depression-era pieces in this dining room a totally new take on life. Instead of appearing antiquated and quaint, the room now enjoys a cutting-edge, retro-chic appeal.

Above: Employing folding slat furniture is an easy and quick way to create an informal dining spot anywhere in a home. Here, bright hues add an element of surprise to the conventional pieces, turning them from routine to stylish, while bold textiles on the table and a checkered sisal rug below enhance the fresh-looking appeal of the space.

Below: AS DEMONSTRATED BY THE USE OF YELLOW AND GREEN IN THIS ARTS AND CRAFTS–STYLE DINING AREA, USING COLOR IS ONE WAY TO ADD INDIVIDUALITY AND WARMTH TO A ROOM WITHOUT ADDING CLUTTER. THE PALE YELLOW IS WELCOMING AND SOFTENS THE SPARE, RECTILINEAR QUALITY OF THE ARCHITECTURE AND ANTIQUE ACACIA DINING TABLE. AT THE SAME TIME, THE COOL DARK GREEN EMPHASIZES THE INTERESTING SHAPES OF THE WINDOW AND DOOR PANES, PROVIDING AN EFFECT THAT IS DISTINCTIVE, UNIQUE, AND HARMONIOUS.

Left: THANKS TO A NOVEL DINING SET THAT COUPLES QUEEN ANNE STYLING WITH BIEDERMEIER STAINS, THIS DINING ROOM IS LOADED WITH CHARACTER. RELAXED WICKER CHAIRS PUNCTUATED WITH BOLDLY PATTERNED PILLOWS CREATE THE SENSATION OF DINING AT A CARIBBEAN RESORT. **Above:** FROM THE BEAMED CEILING TO THE PRIMITIVE MANTEL TO THE PLANKED FLOOR, THIS COUNTRY COTTAGE DINING AREA EMPLOYS A WIDE RANGE OF WOODS. WARM YELLOW WALLS HELP TIE THE SPACE TOGETHER, OFFERING A FLATTERING BACK-DROP FOR THE VARIOUS WOODS AS WELL AS FOR A COLLECTION OF CHINA THAT PICKS UP THE COLORS OF THE TILED FIREPLACE. PAINTED LINES ABOVE THE MANTEL CREATE THE ILLUSION OF PANELS, WHICH APPEAR TO FRAME SMALL GROUPINGS OF THE CHINA.

Combined Dining

Some say that the formal dining room is on the way out, and that its demise can be traced directly to the rise of the eat-in kitchen. Although there may be some truth to this assessment, it certainly does not tell the whole story. Space constraints in general, coupled with contemporary styles of design, have led to the rise of combined dining spaces. An apartment or loft is far less likely to have its own formal dining room. But the home that has a spectacular eat-in kitchen probably also sports a stunning dining room. Formal dining rooms are not necessarily on the way out, but combined dining spaces are definitely "in."

Rooms devoted solely to dining were a luxury when they were first developed in the seventeenth century and are a luxury once again today for those of us who live in

smaller quarters. But this quandary forces us to think creatively. Dining rooms have been combined with living rooms, libraries, family rooms, kitchens, and even game rooms. And these rooms are not necessarily less formal; they are merely resourceful uses of space.

The best combined dining spaces require careful planning in order to work. It is helpful if kitchens close off or have some structural device to signal separation from the eating area, especially since they tend to get messy. And libraries should have ample storage so the space can be quickly converted back and forth. If papers are strewn across a dining table, it is less likely to be used for eating. Despite the fact that a space serves two functions, one should not encroach upon the other.

Opposite: Flat slat paneling gets character and panache with touches of neoclassical styling. Dropped cornice moldings and shallow arches trim the paneling, while Doric columns painted glossy black delineate the dining area. The same lustrous contrast is skillfully integrated into the rest of the space via the window casements.

Above: The narrow passage connecting a kitchen and dining area was resourcefully turned into a mini library with the simple addition of a stocked bookshelf. Combined with a "chalkboard" print and basic wooden furnishings, the books give the dining area a schoolroom feeling.

Left: A DINING AREA WAS CREATED IN THE MIDST OF THIS INDUSTRIAL-STYLE KITCHEN WITH THE INTRODUCTION OF A MASSIVE TABLE THAT MAINTAINS THE ORIGINAL TONE OF THE ROOM WITH ITS LUSTROUS STEEL AND MARBLE. A SUBTLE GRAY PALETTE AND A STRIKING ANGLED LAYOUT ADD STYLE AND GRACE TO THE SETTING.

Opposite: IN THIS VAST GREAT ROOM, A SOARING TWO-STORY SPACE DEFINES THE DINING AREA'S BOUNDARIES, REINFORCED BY A BUILT-IN UNIT THAT CLEVERLY INCORPORATES SEATING FOR THE LIVING ROOM AND STORAGE FOR THE DINING ROOM. ANTIQUES ARE EQUALLY AT HOME WITH CONTEMPORARY PIECES SINCE MOST OF THE FURNISHINGS ARE BASIC AND THE WALLS ARE PURE WHITE. THUS, A QUEEN ANNE DINING SET RESTS EASY NEXT TO THE SLEEK CONTEMPORARY CABINET-CUM-SOFA, WHILE AN INTRICATE VICTORIAN QUILT OFFERS A DAZZLING DISPLAY OF COLOR OVERHEAD.

Right: A MULTIFUNCTIONAL CONTEMPORARY MILIEU CAN STILL HAVE A THOROUGHLY TRADITIONAL APPEAL. IN THIS SETTING, THE DINING ROOM FEATURES A TABLE OF INTRICATE INLAID WOOD FLANKED WITH UPHOLSTERED AND SKIRTED CHAIRS; THE LIVING ROOM IS FURNISHED WITH AN OVERSTUFFED SOFA, ARMCHAIR, AND OTTOMAN; AND THE KITCHEN IS BORDERED BY A NEOCLASSICAL PILASTER AND A SUMPTUOUS MARBLE COUNTERTOP. THANKS TO THE FURNISHINGS, A SENSE OF CONVENTION AND HERITAGE IS PERVASIVE, DESPITE THE CONTEMPORARY OPENNESS OF THE SPACE.

Above: AN OPEN FLOOR PLAN CAN STILL SUPPORT A FORMAL DINING ROOM, AS EVIDENCED BY THIS LOFTLIKE SETTING. WHILE YELLOW AND BLUE UPHOLSTERY GIVES A PLAYFUL LOOK TO THE LIVING AREAS OF THE SPACE, BLACK IMBUES THE DINING AREA WITH AN ELEVATED SENSE OF DECORUM. THE PRECISE LINES OF THE DINING ROOM'S FURNISHINGS PLAY OFF THE SPACE'S AUSTERE ARCHITECTURAL ELEMENTS, INCLUDING THE STARK BLACK SUPPORT BEAMS AND BUILT-IN MINIMALIST SIDEBOARD.

Left: IN THIS CONTEMPORARY LOFT, COLOR BECOMES THE DIVIDER, WITH AN INTENSE SHADE OF TURQUOISE SETTING OFF THE PARTS OF THE SPACE THAT REVOLVE AROUND EATING. THE KITCHEN COUNTER, THE DINING CHAIRS, AND THE WALL ADJACENT TO THE TABLE ARE COVERED WITH THIS HUE, GIVING THESE AREAS AN ENTIRELY DIFFERENT AMBIENCE THAN THE LIVING ROOM BORDERED IN COOL SHADES OF SILVER AND WHITE. THE MELLOW TONES OF THE WOOD SEEN IN THE COLUMNS, TABLE, AND EXPOSED CEILING JOISTS BRING A SOFT GLOW TO THE EATING SPACE.

Opposite: UNOBTRUSIVE PANEL DOORS ALLOW THIS PRISTINE DINING AREA TO BE EITHER FORMAL OR RELAXED IN TONE. WHEN THE DOORS ARE OPEN, THE ECLECTIC FURNISHINGS AND TWO-TONE CARPETING OF THE LIVING AREA INFLUENCE THE DEMEANOR OF THE DINING ROOM, CREATING A MORE CASUAL AMBIENCE. BUT WITH THE DOORS CLOSED, THE DINING AREA TAKES ON A WHOLE DIFFERENT PERSONALITY. IN EITHER CASE, ULTRACONTEMPORARY PIECES PAIRED TOGETHER AS A DINING SET, REGAL PURPLE DRAPES, A POLISHED HARDWOOD FLOOR, AND A FORMAL ARRANGEMENT OF ARTWORK THAT EVOKES CLASSICAL SYMMETRY AND STYLING GIVE THE DINING SPACE A REFINED AIR.

Above: IN A SERENE SETTING WITH PLUSH ART DECO CHAIRS AND AN AMERICAN EMPIRE DINING SET, COLOR IS USED TO ENHANCE THE FORMALITY OF THE TWO ACTIVITY CENTERS. ALTHOUGH THE CARPETING THROUGHOUT IS A MELLOW BEIGE, THE DINING AREA IS SET APART FROM THE LIVING ROOM BY THE DARK TONES OF ITS FURNISHINGS, WHICH PROVIDE DYNAMIC CONTRAST.

Left: AUSTERE PIECES THAT ARE CLASSICS OF MODERN DESIGN DOMINATE THIS COMBINATION LIVING AND DINING ROOM, BUT THE SPACE RETAINS REMARKABLE WARMTH THANKS TO A DIVERSE MIX OF MATERIALS. ORIENTAL CARPETS AND A TRADING BLANKET ARE RADIANT IN DEEP RED WOOL AND WORK WONDERFULLY WITH THE BACKDROP OF ROUGHLY HEWN BRICK. EARTHY WOOD TOUCHES PUNCTUATE THE MIX, AND A COLLECTION OF RICE-PAPER AND PARCHMENT LAMPS CASTS A MELLOW GLOW OVER THE MILIEU. THUS, THE ROOM IS COZY, COMFORTABLE, AND CONTEMPORARY ALL AT THE SAME TIME.

Above: A WOODEN UNIT CONSISTING OF A WORK SURFACE, SHELVES, CABINETS, AND DRAWERS IS BANKED ALONG THE FAR WALL OF THIS ROOM, ALLOWING THE SPACE TO SERVE AS BOTH A DINING ROOM AND A STUDY. STREAMLINED BENEATH A VAST WINDOW, THE WORK SPACE RESTS UNOBTRUSIVELY ALONGSIDE THE DINING AREA, FOR THE OUTDOOR VIEW DRAWS THE DINER'S EYE BEYOND THE UNIT. THE DESK CHAIR, WHICH IS REALLY PART OF THE DINING SET, CAN TRAVEL FREELY BETWEEN THE TWO AREAS TO PERFORM ITS SERVICE WHERE IT IS NEEDED MOST.

Opposite: It is sensible to make an eating space flexible, as in this consummate kitchen-cum-dining room. The kitchen island and dining room table, which are made of the same sumptuous materials (namely granite and stainless steel), can be left to practically blend into each other or can be separated by sliding wooden panels that close off each room and give the dining area a more formal character. The same amber wood veneers cover the cabinets in both areas to unify the space. **Above, left:** Shining surfaces and forceful shapes make an awkward setup elegant in this kitchen and dining area. A stairway that bisects the space could have been a liability, but in glossy black metal topped with highly polished wood, it is a stunning sculptural focal point that also manages to give each separate area a sense of definition. A gleaming glass table, silvery walls, and shining steel surfaces in the kitchen all play off one another, while creamy and curvy molded chairs soften the space. **Above, right:** Shrouded in white, various materials such as wood slats, ceramic tiles, and Formica countertops seem unified in this intricate, multilevel kitchen. Meanwhile, wood furnishings in different tones set off the dining area, supplying it with its own identity. Although the decorative elements of this superbly designed space run the gamut from contemporary to country, they all fit together like the pieces of a complex jigsaw puzzle.

Below: THIS IS TRULY A ROOM DESIGNED FOR ENTERTAINING. AFTER ENJOYING A SAVORY MEAL AND SCINTILLATING CONVERSATION AT THE DINNER TABLE, RESIDENTS AND GUESTS ALIKE CAN SLIP OVER TO THE POOL TABLE FOR MORE FUN. EVEN THE DECOR ITSELF, WITH ITS ECLECTIC BLEND OF BOLDLY PAINTED WALLS, EARTHY BASKETS, ETHNIC ARTWORKS, ITALIAN POTTERY, AND PROVINCIAL FURNITURE, IS A SOURCE OF ENTERTAINMENT, PROVIDING A FASCINATING VISUAL DIVERSION AND SPARKING CONVERSATION.

Above: COUNTRY KITSCH REIGNS SUPREME IN THIS EAT-IN-KITCHEN, WHICH WOULD PROBABLY BE QUITE ORDINARY SANS THE COLORFUL PAINT JOB. COLONIAL CABINETS HAVE BEEN PRETTIED UP WITH SUNFLOWERS AGAINST A VIBRANT TEAL BLUE, WHILE THE WOOD FLOOR HAS BEEN DECKED OUT WITH A BUSY STENCILED DESIGN IN COMPLEMENTARY HUES. A PRACTICALLY INVISIBLE GLASS TABLE WAS CHOSEN AS THE DINING SURFACE SO AS NOT TO DETRACT FROM THE BOISTEROUS PLACE SETTINGS AND THE WHIMSICAL CHAIRS, WHICH ARE TAKEOFFS ON CLASSIC COUNTRY HITCHCOCKS.

Above: ATTRACTIVE TILING SPORTING A FLORAL BORDER AND CENTRAL FLORAL DESIGN NOT ONLY MAKES A BEAUTIFUL BACKDROP IN THIS EAT-IN KITCHEN, BUT IT ALSO TRICKS THE EYE. AT FIRST GLANCE, THE RIGHT WALL LOOKS LIKE A MASSIVE BREAKFRONT, THANKS TO A MASTERFUL ARRANGEMENT OF TILES AND METICULOUSLY ARTICULATED CABINETS; IN ACTUALITY, THOUGH, THE SETUP MERELY CONSISTS OF A KITCHEN COUNTER COUPLED WITH BUILT-INS. THE TILES ALSO PROVIDE ACCENTS OF GREEN THAT COORDINATE WITH THE WICKER CHAIRS AND DOOR TRIM, ADDING WELCOME DEPTH TO THE ALMOST ENTIRELY YELLOW SURROUNDINGS.

EATING ALFRESCO

There is nothing like fresh air for stimulating an appetite, or the beauty of a dazzling landscape for setting a scene. Savoring the wonders of nature and a marvelous repast simultaneously enhances the art of dining and lends a sense of adventure to a meal. And since dining alfresco is not recognized as part of the usual routine, it is often viewed as a special event or treat.

Interestingly enough, the great outdoors actually preceded the dining room as a formal place to hold a repast. Since most homes were very small and did not have rooms devoted solely to dining, outdoor areas were reserved for more formal meals. When feasts were prepared for special occasions, they were staged in a deco-

rous fashion outside. In fact, picnics were derived from the lavish banquets held outdoors during the sixteenth century, becoming less formal over time to the point where they lost their tables and chairs.

Today, eating outdoors remains a staged event, though not necessarily a formal affair. While some outdoor dining areas are temporary setups, such as a simple table and chairs in a grassy clearing, others are more permanent, consisting of pieces that remain on a patio or balcony year-round. In any case, the furnishings can be dressed up or down to accommodate meals of different levels of decorum. Although an outdoor setting is usually remarkable to begin with, the actual trappings have great power to enhance the dining experience.

Opposite: INSTEAD OF THE AIRY, PASTORAL FEELING IMPARTED BY SIMILAR PIECES COATED IN WHITE, THIS BLACK PATIO SET GIVES OFF AN AIR OF SLICK URBAN SOPHISTICATION. PERHAPS THE MOST STRIKING ELEMENT OF THE DECOR IS THE CHANDELIER, WHICH, WITH ITS UNUSUAL BLACK CANDLES, IS POSITIVELY BEWITCHING.

Above: IN THE MIDST OF A HEAVILY WOODED LOT, AN IMPECCABLY GROOMED WHITEWASHED PORCH MAKES A GREAT PLACE TO EAT. FILLING IT WITH THESE ADIRONDACK-STYLE TWIG FURNISHINGS IS LIKE A DOUBLE ENTENDRE: THE KNOTTY LINES OF THE PIECES PLAY OFF THE GNARLED TREES TO MAKE THE POLISHED PORCH SEEM RUSTIC, WHILE PRISTINE WHITE CUSHIONS EMBELLISHED WITH IVY CAUSE THE PENDULUM TO SWING BACK THE OTHER WAY BY ADDING A TOUCH OF REFINEMENT.

Left: A CITYSCAPE CAN BE JUST AS APPEALING AS A GORGEOUS GARDEN, ESPECIALLY IF THE SCENE IS AS CHARMING AS THE ONE OFFERED BY THESE BEAUX ARTS BUILDINGS. A TINY LITTLE TABLE FOR TWO, WHICH IS CUTE BUT CERTAINLY NOT NOTABLE ON ITS OWN, BECOMES OVER-WHELMINGLY ROMANTIC AND WIN-SOME WEDGED INTO THIS NARROW ROOFTOP BALCONY. A BLUE-AND-WHITE CHECKED TABLECLOTH CON-TRIBUTES TO THE QUAINT LOOK.

Opposite: DESPITE THE POLISH AND GRANDEUR OF THIS COURTYARD, A MODEST METAL TABLE-AND-CHAIR SET FITS RIGHT IN. THE DELICATE, CURVING LINES OF THE CHAIRS SOFTEN THE AUSTERITY OF THE METAL, WHILE A FULL-LENGTH COVERING WRAPS THE TABLE IN ELEGANCE. WITH ITS SWIRLING VINE MOTIF, THE TABLECLOTH ECHOES THE GRACEFUL LINES OF THE CHAIRS, GIVING THE ENTIRE SETUP A SENSE OF HARMONY.

Right: THIS SPACIOUS VERANDA HAS BEEN INGENIOUSLY TRANS-FORMED INTO AN ARRESTING OUTDOOR DINING ROOM WITH THE HELP OF EYE-CATCHING TEXTILES. BOLD BLACK-AND-WHITE STRIPED PIECES OF FABRIC ARE SUSPENDED BETWEEN THE COLUMNS TO BECOME DAZZLING "WALLS" THAT SUPPLY PRIVACY AS WELL AS SHELTER FROM THE ELEMENTS. MOREOVER, THESE DARING TEXTILES OFFER A HUGE DOSE OF GLAMOUR TO THE SETUP.

Left: Conventions seem to dissolve when we blend the great outdoors with dining. Forget the usual trappings of formality; here, tropical foliage fills in for walls, and a thatched overhang supplants the ceiling. The "proper" Regency furnishings seem fanciful instead of stiff, and the icy marble floor looks like a refreshing oasis.

Above: A spectacular veranda, rife with such arresting architectural details as soaring columns and an artfully trussed ceiling, is a perfect place to dine. Painted white, it is like a blank slate that can take on any look depending upon how it is accessorized. In this case, simple canvas slipcovers in white give the stately setting a pure, relaxed look. Slipcovers are not only an effective means of hiding undesirable upholstery and unifying mismatched pieces, they are, above all else, an inexpensive way to achieve an exquisite look.

Opposite: THE NOVEL BACKS OF THE CHAIRS IN THIS DINING ROOM DEFTLY ECHO THE PICKET FENCE OUTSIDE, WHICH SQUARES OFF A TINY GARDEN. WHEN THE FRENCH DOORS ARE OPEN, THE TWO AREAS BECOME ONE, OWING TO THE EARTHY MATERIALS USED TO PAVE BOTH AS WELL AS THE HARMONIOUS PAIRING OF GOLDEN WOOD FURNISHINGS WITH THE BRICK PATIO. **Below:** IT IS POSSIBLE TO CAPITALIZE ON ANY GORGEOUS OPEN-AIR NOOK FOR ALFRESCO DINING. HERE, A CHARMING LITTLE CORNER OF A PORCH MAKES A PERFECT SPOT FOR EATING OUTDOORS. FURNISHED WITH AN EASY CHAIR, A ROCKER, AND A LOW-SLUNG CHECKERBOARD TABLE, THE SETTING IS IDEAL FOR A RELAXED LUNCH OR SNACK. AN ABUNDANCE OF GREENERY GIVES THE SPACE AN AIR OF SECLUSION.

Above: THANKS TO FRENCH DOORS, WHICH CAN BE FLUNG OPEN TO LET THE GLORIES BEYOND STREAM IN, IT IS POSSIBLE TO ENJOY THE PLEASURES OF DINING ALFRESCO INDOORS. HERE, WHIMSICAL FURNISHINGS COMPLEMENT AN EQUALLY FANCIFUL GARDEN. DELICATE VICTORIAN-STYLE WIRE CHAIRS THAT LOOK LIKE THEY CAME OUT OF AN ICE CREAM PARLOR ARE THE PERFECT COUNTERPOINTS TO A SUBSTANTIAL, BUT EQUALLY ORNATE, MARBLE-TOPPED TABLE. OUTSIDE, A TINY PATIO TABLE MADE OUT OF SIMILAR MATERIALS SUBTLY TIES THE TWO SPACES TOGETHER.

Above: COLUMNS ARE PERENNIAL CATALYSTS, CAPABLE OF WORKING MAGIC ON THE HUMBLEST FURNISHINGS AND RAISING THEM TO HIGHER LEVELS. HERE, THESE MAJESTIC ARCHITECTURAL ELEMENTS TRANSFORM A STRAIGHTFORWARD STONE PATIO, MODESTLY APPOINTED WITH A CEDAR SLAT TABLE AND BENCH, DIRECTOR'S CHAIRS, AND A CANVAS UMBRELLA, INTO A HIGHLY REFINED MILIEU. AND SIMPLE FOLIAGE, WHICH BECOMES LUSH USED EN MASSE, SOFTENS THE HARD-EDGED LINES OF THE PIECES, ADDING TO THE SETTING'S LUXURIOUS TONE. **Opposite:** POOLSIDE DINING IN THIS CAPTIVATING SPOT IS AN UPLIFTING AFFAIR, THANKS TO BRIGHTLY COLORED CUSHIONS THAT SERVE AS ENERGIZING ACCENTS AGAINST THE TERRA-COTTA BACKGROUND. THE BEAUTY OF THE POOL DOES THE REST, IMBUING THE SETTING WITH SERENITY.

Left: SENSIBLE CEDAR FURNITURE THAT CAN BE LEFT OUT ALL YEAR LONG IS A GREAT CHOICE FOR A SOLID BRICK PATIO. TOGETHER, THE CEDAR AND BRICK EXUDE STRENGTH AND SUBSTANCE AS THEY STAND UP TO THE ELEMENTS. POTTED ANNUALS IN VIVID COLORS LIVEN UP THE EARTHY HUES, WHILE A VIVID FLORAL CLOTH GIVES THE TABLE A FESTIVE AIR.

Opposite: A MERE CLEARING, COMPLETE WITH GRAVEL AND DIRT UNDERFOOT, GOES FROM UNPRETEN-TIOUS TO ENCHANTING THANKS TO ACCESSORIES THAT DEFTLY ENHANCE THE SETTING'S NATURAL ATTRIBUTES. FOUR WHITE FOLDING CHAIRS, ACCENTED BY TWO CHAIRS THAT ARE A BIT MORE BAROQUE, MIRROR THE AIRY FEELING OF THE OUTDOORS, WHILE A PINK-AND-WHITE CHECKED TABLECLOTH ECHOES THE LOCA-TION'S NATURAL COLOR SCHEME.

SOURCES

DESIGNERS

(page 6)
Tom Beeton
Los Angeles, CA
(310) 657-5600

(page 8)
Hutton Wilkinson
Los Angeles, CA
(213) 874-7760

(page 10)
Robert Curry
New York, NY
(212) 206-0505

(pages 12, 28, 37 left, 45, 65)
Jarrett Hedborg
Wall paintings by Nancy
    Kinisch
Los Angeles, CA
(310) 271-1437

(page 13)
Francois Theise
Adesso Furniture
Boston, MA
(617) 451-2212

(page 14)
Roy McMakin
Seattle, WA
(206) 323-6992

(pages 15, 34)
Denise Domergue
Los Angeles, CA
(310) 453-7717

(page 16)
Heidi Wianecki
Los Angeles, CA
(310) 459-5550

(page 17)
Janet Schirn Design Group
Chicago, IL
(312) 222-0017

(pages 18 top, 67)
Tessa Kennedy
London, England
071 221 4546

(page 18, bottom)
Tom Callaway
Los Angeles, CA
(310) 828-1030

(page 19)
Goodman/Charlton
Los Angeles, CA
(310) 657-7068

(page 20)
John Kulhanek
Los Angeles, CA
(310) 474-6722

(page 21)
Diane Thompson
Modern Living
Los Angeles, CA
(213) 655-3898

(page 23)
Joel Chen
Los Angeles, CA
(213) 655-6310

(pages 24 bottom, 54)
Tanys Langdon, architect
Chicago, IL
(312) 282-2144

(page 25)
Lee Harris Pomeroy Associates
New York, NY
(212) 334-2600

(page 32, right)
Barbara Barry
Los Angeles, CA
(310) 276-9977

(page 33)
Janice McCarthy
Los Angeles, CA
(213) 651-4229
(818) 793-9130

(page 35, left)
Tom Catalano
Boston, MA
(617) 338-6447

(pages 35 right, 46 left)
Brian Murphy
Santa Monica, CA
(310) 459-0955

(page 39)
Peter Bohlin, architect
Philadelphia, PA
(215) 592-0600

(page 40, left)
Anita Calero
New York, NY
(212) 727-8949

(page 41)
Richar Interiors
Chicago, IL
(312) 951-0924

(page 42)
Charles Riley
New York, NY
(212) 206-8395

(page 44)
John Gillespie, architect
Camden, MN
(207) 236-8054

(page 46, right)
Lindsay Boutrous-Ghali
Lindsay Associates
Boston, MA
(617) 262-1948

(page 47)
Bob Knight, architect
Blue Hill, MN
(207) 374-2845

(page 48)
Larry Totah
Los Angeles, CA
(310) 453-8888

(page 49)
Reiter & Reiter
Boston, MA
(617) 965-0289

(page 50)
C & J Katz Studio
Boston, MA 02114
(617) 367-0537

(page 52)
Herman Miller for the Home
Zeeland, MI
(800) 646-4400

(page 55, left)
Mulder/Katkov
Los Angeles, CA
(310) 391-0680

(page 55, right)
Tom Bosworth
Seattle, WA
(206) 522-5549

(page 57)
Laura Clayton Baker
Los Angeles, CA
(310) 573-1232

(page 58)
Penny Bianchi
Los Angeles, CA
(213) 682-1487

(page 59)
Sarah Kaltman
New York, NY
(212) 721-6497

(page 61)
Annie Kelly
Los Angeles, CA
(213) 876-8030

(page 64, left)
Michel Pouliot, artist
Dorchester, MA
(617) 265-7576

(page 64, right)
P.J. Wheeler Associates
Boston, MA
(617) 426-5921

(page 68)
Patricia O'Shaunesey
New York, NY
(212) 674-2833

PHOTOGRAPHY CREDITS

© Judith Bromley: 24 bottom, 26, 54
© Tria Giovan: 40 left, 42–43, 59, 68
© Annet Held/Arcaid: 60 top
© David Livingston: 29
© Richard Mandelkorn: 46 bottom
© Nick Merrick/Hedrich-Blessing: 52
© Michael Mundy: 2, 22, 24 top, 30, 31
© Mary Nichols: 17
© David Phelps: 37 bottom, 40 right, 60 bottom
© Eric Roth: 13, 38, 50, 51, 56 top, 64 both

© Tim Street-Porter: 8, 12, 14 left, 18 both, 28, 32 both (32 left, designed by Bob and Isabel Higgins), 35 right, 36 (designed by Mark and Margo Werts, Los Angeles, CA), 37 top, 43 top (home of Pauline Morton, Los Angeles, CA), 45, 46 top, 48, 53, 58, 61, 62–63 (Grounds Kent Architects, Perth, Australia), 65, 67, 69 (designed by Ron Hefler, West Hollywood, CA)
© Brian Vanden Brink: 10, 11, 27, 35 left, 39, 44, 47, 49
© Dominique Vorillon: 6, 14–15, 16, 19, 20, 21, 23, 33, 34, 43 bottom, 55 both, 56 bottom, 57, 63 right
© Paul Warchol: 25
© Jean Wright/Arcaid: 66 (Deece Giles, Architect, Sidney, Australia)
© James Yochum: 41

INDEX